Hello.

the secret me book

a journal to celebrate
what makes you, *you*

Rachel Kempster

Meg Leder

sourcebooks

Published by Sourcebooks, Inc.
P.O. Box 4410, Naperville, Illinois 60567-4410
(630) 961-3900
Fax: (630) 961-2168
www.sourcebooks.com

Library of Congress Cataloging-in-Publication Data

Kempster, Rachel.
  The secret me book : what makes you, you? / Rachel Kempster and Meg Leder.
    p. cm.
  (pbk. : alk. paper) 1. Self-actualization (Psychology) 2. Self. 3. Thought and thinking. I. Leder, Meg. II. Title.
  BF637.S4K4496 2012
  158.1—dc23
                                        2011039421

Printed and bound in the United States of America.
VP 10 9 8 7 6 5 4 3 2 1

To mom (my biggest
fan on earth) and dad (my
biggest fan in the hereafter)

—Rachel

To Jim and Pat Leder,
for making me, me, and for Mary
Mitchell, for being a gem.

—Meg

INTRODUCTION

Laying in bed at night, what do you think about?

When you wish upon a star, what is the thing you hope for time and time again?

Who are your soul mates, the people who understand your inner workings more than anyone else?

What writing or lyrics speak to you as if your mirror-self wrote them?

Your answers to these questions are most likely different from everyone else's in the entire world. And considering there are a lot of us out there, that's saying something!

But it's these answers—the things that make you tick and hum, the imprecise combination of quirks and habits that are yours and yours alone— that make you who you are, that make up what Rachel and I like to call your secret self. Think of it like your soul's own precise and particular fingerprint, something that is constant no matter where you are or who you're with.

In *The Secret Me Book*, you'll learn about this part of you in a deeper, more meaningful way.

Why, you may wonder, do I want to learn more about myself? Let me share a story about my own secret self…

2010 wasn't one of my favorite years. I went through some personal stuff that left me reeling, and I had to have my wonderful fourteen-year-old cat Baxter put to sleep. There were times I felt so completely gut-sad that all I could manage to focus on was the rise and fall of my ribs as the breath came in and out.

But here's the thing about being alone: you begin to learn what you are made of. You discover there's a rhythm to your breathing, strength in your bones. That year, I found in myself a current running deep—like a secret underground river—silent and steady and strong. It's mysterious, this dark river, but it's constant and true, as sure as the breath I take in. I like to think it's the real me—the secret me.

So who is this secret me, *my* secret me? It's someone who believes books are a first home—that they can take me outside of my mind, to places that are beautiful and strange. It's someone who cultivates friendships with people who are witty and kind and dependable—who will take me roller-skating when I'm sad, even if it's a two-hour commute. It's someone who believes in comfort food: a plate of rice and beans with freshly chopped tomatoes and cilantro, or a burger from the Ear Inn. It's someone who can seek out music for my moods—the Magnetic Fields for when I'm heartbroken, Patty Griffin when I need solace.

My secret self is the same whether I'm in a crowd of people or alone in my apartment. It's who I am when I'm in the middle of fresh heartbreak, but it's also me when I believe I'll find love again. It's me when I've lost my best cat buddy, but it's also me when I've taken in a new punk-ass kitten. It is the constant part of me I can always count on—my true self.

What makes up *your* secret self?

This book is about recognizing who you were, who you are, who you wish to be. It's not about self-help or self-improvement—rather it's about self-recognition…getting to know and trust and rely upon the core parts of you.

As you move through these pages, you'll find prompts to spark your thoughts, quotes to inspire you, and what we have dubbed Secret Surveys—quick glimpses at the secret selves of those around us.

By looking at the things you keep in the dark, you'll tap into secret parts of you in a deeper way, learning to celebrate what you usually keep quiet and unspoken. You'll discover what you're made of: the strength that will carry you through days of joy and spring, days of heartbreak and loss, days of the ordinary.

You'll discover what makes you, *you*.

We wish you the best of luck on your journey.

HOW TO USE *THE SECRET ME BOOK*

This is your book, which means you can do *whatever* you want with it:

* Share it, or keep it totally secret.
* Go in order, or skip around to your heart's content.
* Respond to the prompts as they are, edit away, or cross 'em out and write down your own.
* Use markers or pencils or crayons or paint or invisible ink.
* Write in print or cursive. Write in straight lines or upside down. Or follow the lead of Jane Austen, who'd write letters by writing lines from left to right, and then would write lines on top of those, from top to bottom.
* Enjoy the cover and face it out on your bookshelf. Or cover the whole thing with a brown grocery bag (school textbook style), and redesign it so it's yours.

No rules for this one…just to do what you want. Because it's all about your secret self, and in these pages, your secret self can run free!*

*Or skip. Or jump.
Or sit very still on
a park bench.
Or go wave jumping at the local beach.
Your call.

"I took a deep breath and listened to the old bray of my heart. I am. I am. I am."

—Sylvia Plath, *The Bell Jar*

hen are you most truly yourself?

Map your childhood neighborhood. Include your favorite haunts and hideaways, where your best friends lived, and the home that gave out the best candy for Halloween.

Consider the five most _____ moments of your life. Record them here, and examine them like a scientist. Spend some time looking for patterns (are they spread evenly over the life you've lived?) and differences (has what made you happy changed over time) and connections.

HAPPY

SAD

SCARY

VULNERABLE

FUNNY

> When I was a kid, I desperately wanted the back of my closet to open up into Narnia. I also believed that the meadow in the field at the top of our hill was magic and that we could truly conjure the ghosts of George Washington and Elvis during "séances."
>
> —Meg

WHERE DO YOU FIND YOUR VERSION OF MAGIC?

> "After being in *Harry Potter*, I believe a bit more in magic than I did before."
>
> —Rupert Grint

In Philip Pullman's Golden Compass books, the characters all have daemons—animal manifestations of their inner selves. What would your daemon be? Draw it here.

What's that tattoo you've always wanted, even if you never get it? Draw potential designs (or phrases) here.

The state of my fridge is a good indicator of the state of my life. Right now it's kind of empty and a mess—there's an expired bit of goat cheese, condiments, and a half-drunk can of Pepsi Max. This means that I've been too busy to shop or cook. This also means I've been eating far too much chicken and rice from the King of Falafel for dinner every night. ·

—Rachel

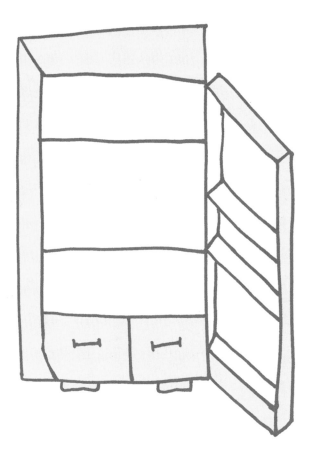

Take a look at what's in your fridge now. What story does it tell about the state of your life right now?

In the classic film *The Odd Couple*, two friends become accidental roommates. Felix is the picture of fastidiousness—a hyper organized, sensitive neatnik who vacuums the curtains, dusts his knickknacks, and sets the dinner table in a way that would make Martha Stewart proud. Oscar is his opposite—a messy fellow who props his feet up on the table, eats sloppy sandwiches without a plate, and waits to do laundry until he's down to his last pair of pants.

Most of us aren't quite that extreme—we're a little bit Oscar and a little bit Felix. Use this space to list the ways you're a Felix or an Oscar. Which character suits you best? Has that changed for you over time, or have you always preferred rumpled clothes to ironing?

OSCAR	FELIX

Is there something you daydream about again and again? Write about it here.

"I was trying to daydream, but my mind kept wandering."

— Steven Wright

My grandmother made heaps of yummy things, but there was one thing in particular that I loved: frozen peaches. I realize that frozen peaches doesn't sound much like a treasured family dish, but believe me, they were magic. Each August, the height of peach season, Grandma would buy baskets of peaches from Davis's Peach Farm. She'd wash them, peel them, slice them, and then sprinkle them with sugar and lemon juice and a pinch of secret ingredients. Finally, she'd seal them up and freeze bags and bags and bags of the sweet peaches so we'd have them until the next August when she'd make some more.

—Rachel

What family recipes do you cherish? Why?
Include the recipe here:

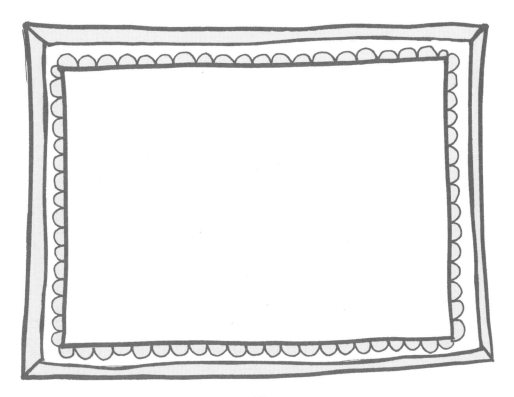

It's no myth that people make confessions to bartenders and hairdressers—it happens all day long. Why do you think people bare their souls to strangers? Is it something that you've ever done or would consider doing? What would you say?

One of my big indulgences is a fancy haircut and color at Arrojo, a salon near my office. I love the ritual of getting my hair washed and dyed and snipped and styled in a completely fun and relaxing space. But I also love catching up with Courtney and Lee, the magicians who make my hair pretty. I end up telling them all kinds of things I should keep to myself—there's something about the soothing hum of the blow dryers that makes me inordinately indiscrete.

—Rachel

Arachnophobia (fear of spiders), acrophobia (fear of heights), coulrophobia (fear of clowns)—what is the thing YOU fear the most? Where did the fear originate? Have you been able to conquer it? Or does something stand in your way? Does everyone know to turn off *Footloose* before you come into the room because you're chorophobic (afraid of dancing), or do you keep your fears to yourself? Why?

hat do you see when you shut your eyes? Record it here.

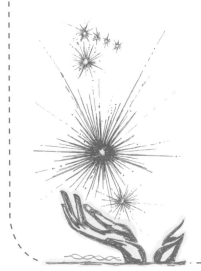

"I shut my eyes in order to see."

—Paul Gauguin

The meaning of the word "altar" changes from religion to religion, from time to time. Altars are places for ceremony, devotion, and reflection. In that spirit, make yourself a tabletop altar to something dear—whether it be squirrels or your family or favorite *American Idol* contestant. Search Flickr for "altar," and you'll be inspired by the mix of traditional and creative altars on display. Some are sparse—a simple verse and a vase of flowers. Some are elaborate displays of art objects, incense, photos, and more.

Sketch out your plans for your altar below and then make it. You can find inspiration by looking at the Crafty Chica's website: craftychica.blogspot.com.

My friend and neighbor Amy is one of the most level-headed people I know. The crack in her sensible armor? Cadbury Mini-eggs. She's obsessed with them, buying bags at a time, scoping out remaining stock at stores right before Easter, and lamenting when they're finally gone for the season. And when she talks about them, she's rhapsodic, describing the crunch of the shell, the creaminess of the chocolate, the all-around satisfying experience of eating them.

—Meg

WHAT ARE YOU COMPLETELY AND UTTERLY DEVOTED TO? CHRONICLE YOUR PASSION/OBSESSION HERE.

You found the golden ticket! Something spectacular happens, and you have enough money to spend the rest of your life doing whatever you want to do.

Who do you call first?

What's the first thing you'd buy?

Would you give a portion of the money away? Who would you give it to? Now plot out your first week in rich detail below.

Once you've answered for yourself, ask two of your friends to answer the same questions. Do their answers surprise you?

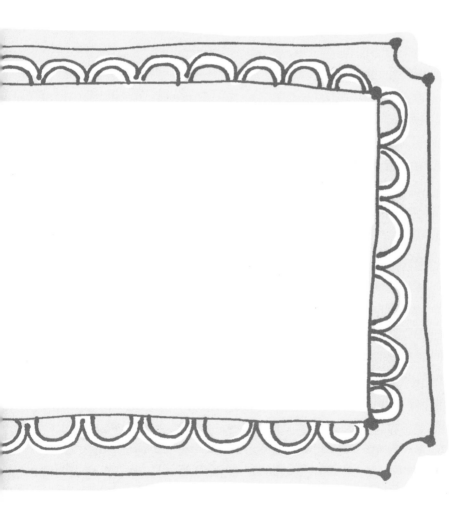

Are there conversations in your life you wish you could have had? A talk with your brother about staying out of trouble in school? One more chance to tell your aunt how much her letters meant to you before she passed away? List the conversations you wish you could have had with the important people in your life. Then list the conversations you still can have. Make one happen.

"Nobody puts Baby in the corner."

— Dirty Dancing

Was there a movie moment in your childhood that stuck with you always? Describe the scene here, and then spend some time thinking about why it had such an impact on you.

When Johnny Castle pulled Baby out of the corner in *Dirty Dancing*, I swooned. Was there anything more dramatic and romantic? I spent most of high school waiting for my own personal Patrick Swayze to invite me out from behind the kitchen table and make me do the lift. Alas, it never happened.

— Rachel

The lyrics for the Indigo Girls song "Virginia Woolf" are a testament to the power words can have over us. In the song, the singer relays how she discovered Virginia Woolf's published diaries, and how the writer's voice was like hearing from a friend. Through these words, the singer finds solace and comfort: "So I know I'm all right, life will come and life will go." What books have found you when you needed them? Who seems to be writing letters to your soul? What are they saying?

» » SECRET SURVEY! « «

WHICH BOOK FOUND YOU WHEN YOU NEEDED IT?

The River Why by James Duncan. —Tracey K.

The Hitchhiker's Guide to the Galaxy by Douglas Adams, which I read one night while grounded in high school. Ended up being thoroughly entertained, which I don't think is what my parents had in mind for me! —Amy H.

James and the Giant Peach, when I was a girl who wanted to escape. —Amy V.

The Girl's Guide to Hunting and Fishing by Melissa Bank. The writing is so incredibly real, and I felt like the story was about me—future me. —Katie L.

A Fan's Note, by Fred Exley —Jack H.

My mom gave me her copy of *Little Women* when I was in sixth grade. How I loved all the characters and even named my daughter after them—Meg! —Pat L.

Candy Freak by Steve Almond—it got me through labor. —Alice P.

Anne of Green Gables, eighth grade, saved my life, let me see someone who was lovable *because* of her quirks. —Candace M.

Greek Gods by John Green —Maxwell R.

The Beauty Myth by Naomi Wolf. I found it on the library shelf when I was nineteen, and it literally changed my entire world view of what it meant to be a woman and an advertisement demographic. —Jessica C.

NOTE: The Harry Potter series, *Anne of Green Gables*, and *Pinkalicious* were big favorites with our secret survey takers.

While Geena Davis is known for her acting skills, she's also a talented archer. Comedian and writer Steve Martin is an expert banjo player. What are your secret talents?

You've got secret talents, but if you could have one new talent you don't have now, what would it be? Write about it here—and write about why you want to be a better artist, cook, writer, singer, carpenter, or anything else your imagination can muster.

C hronicle the development of you. Gather a set of photos of you from throughout your life, and organize them chronologically across the next two pages.

"Do I contradict myself?
Very well then I contradict myself.
(I am large, I contain multitudes.)"

—Walt Whitman

What stories make up your family lore? Chronicle the secret histories of your relatives.

My Grandpa Connor loves to share stories of his growing-up—stories that include brick fights with the local neighborhood kids and jumping from roof to roof of adjoining houses (it's a miracle he made it to adulthood). I love the story he tells about going to dances at Ault Park—a beautiful outdoor pavilion—and how he spent many an evening dancing with the three oldest Burke sisters (a family of six sisters who lived in the neighborhood). When he got back from the war in 1945, he went back to the dances, surprised to find that the youngest Burke sister—Dolores—the one who had watched from the sidelines all those years—had grown up into a beautiful young woman. He started dancing with her, and that's how my grandparents fell in love.

—Meg

n the film *Groundhog Day*, Bill Murray's character gets to redo the same day over and over until he gets it right.

Is there a day you wish you could do over? Describe it here.

If you could be anyone from any time or place, who would you be? Create a fictional alter ego. Give yourself a name, a home, a life. Imagine a new self.

"One's real life is often the life that one does not lead."

—Oscar Wilde

"Two roads diverged in a yellow wood…"

—Robert Frost

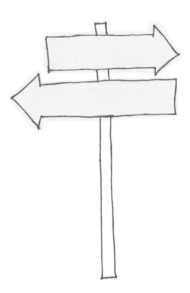

List the key decision moments that made you who you are today. What might have happened if you had taken the other path?

A few days before my dad passed away, he started telling everyone in earshot that he was going to buy a Corvette. "Blue or red," he said, "but I'll let your mother decide the color." He was delighted and emphatic and very, very happy. Later, I learned he had wanted a blue Corvette for years, but life and kids and work got in the way.

—Rachel

What's your blue Corvette? Is there something you can start to do right now to make it a reality in the next week? The next month? The next year?

Use this space to write a letter to yourself at age 9.
What words of wisdom would you share with yourself?

Use this space to write a letter to yourself at age 99. What do you hope you've accomplished? Who do you hope you still know and love?

You're blowing out the candles on your birthday cake. What do you wish for?

You found a stray eyelash, and when you blow it off your finger, you can make a wish. What do you wish for?

You get the lucky end of the wishbone. What do you wish for?

You see a falling star. What do you wish for?

✸✸✸✸✸✸✸

» » SECRET SURVEY! « «

WHAT DO YOU WISH FOR?

That my grandchildren grow up happy. —Karen K.

A new house for my family in Tucson, Arizona. —Max R.

To go to Disney World with my parents. —Mona C.

The confidence to be kind. —Jenny C.

That my nephew will grow up happy and healthy and make a positive difference in the world. —Anita B.

That my brother was still alive. —Jack H.

A chocolate bunny that goes hopping. —Sloane P.

To always be loved. —Mindy F.

To be with my family. —Delaney K.

A million Barbies. —Rebecca N.

To find a four-leaf clover. —Clara L.

Understanding. Or a happy future. (To me, these are intertwined and may really be the same thing.) —Curt G.

To find a million dollars. —Donovan K.

To turn into a Transformer. —Avery D.

I wish that everything was made of candy. —Claire B

True love…still. —Jessica C.

Have you broken any hearts? List them here.

Have you had your heart broken? Write about it here.

When I was in fourth grade, I wrote a six-page, handwritten letter to Sally Ride. I told her how much I admired her for being the first woman astronaut, and then I shared a short story about finding aliens on Mars that I'd written expressly for her. I spent a solid week working on that letter, and it paid off when I got an answer back. It came in a thick envelope along with an autographed picture and some fun space-related activity sheets. I can't imagine ever getting a better piece of mail.

—Rachel

Write a letter to someone you admire—whether they're famous or a friend. Use this space to get your thoughts straight.

Use this page to chronicle your closest friends over time, from toddler-hood to present day. Who are the constants? Who have you lost touch with? What do your friends at different times reflect about you?

In the movie *Zombieland*, Woody Harrelson's character searches high and low for a Twinkie—in a post-apocalyptic America overrun with the living dead, those cream-filled snack cakes become his own personal Holy Grail.

When the world ends and the shock of being the last person alive wears off, what simple pleasures would you search high and low for? Twinkies, hot showers, cold Coca-Cola, vanilla-scented candles?

What odd and particular moments make you laugh and laugh? What things are individual and humorous to you and your friends?

My first New Year's Eve in New York City, my college roommate Amy came to visit. I was eager to show off the quirkiness of the city, and NYC obliged: Riding the subway home in the early hours of 2003, we witnessed a nicely dressed young man caressing a raw steak, placing it in a plastic bag, laying his head down upon the bag, and then singing softly, "We have a bag for our meat. We have a bag for our meat." Amy and I laughed for hours afterward, and even now, when one of us sings the strange lyrics, we both immediately lose it.

—Meg

> "Our bodies are apt to be our autobiographies."
>
> —Gelett Burgess

What are the constellations of your body? What are the particular watermarks that make you, you? A chicken pox scar between your eyebrows, freckles in the shape of a triangle on your arm, the particular shape of the crook of your nose, a series of bumps on the ridge of your left ear? Chronicle them here.

Now, be kind to yourself and compliment your best bits here.

If you could create your perfect hideaway right now, the place you could seek out whenever you needed to escape and relax from your current life, where would it be—Prague? The moon? The Dingle Peninsula? What would it look like? A cottage? A treehouse? Would anyone else know where it was? Your best friend? Your cat? Your niece? No one?

Record the details here.

"Frogs and snails
And puppy-dogs' tails,
That's what little boys are made of.
Sugar and spice
And everything nice,
That's what little girls are made of."

WHAT ARE YOU MADE OF?
COMPOSE A LIST OF THE INGREDIENTS.

C onduct a random survey among friends, family members, and even strangers, and ask them for one word or phrase to describe you. Record the results here.

When an adult asked a younger you what you'd like to be when you grow up, chances are you answered a cowboy or princess or astronaut. Remember what it was like to be enthusiastic and five years old and blissfully unaware of the practical considerations of your future employment (astronauts need 20/20 vision; middle managers make more than cowboys)? What did you want to be? Why?

» » SECRET SURVEY! « «

WHAT DO/DID YOU WANT TO BE
WHEN YOU GROW/GREW UP?

I want to be a voice actor. Or a Broadway singer if only I was more coordinated. Mostly voice actor. —Kerry S.

A veterinarian! (Large animal preferably. I wanted to help cows give birth.) —Kendra H.

An archeologist and a geologist. I still dig rocks (figuratively, not literally). —Alice P.

According to my mom, a go-go dancer or an Avon lady. According to me, a flight attendant, writer, special-ed teacher. –Candace M.

A daddy. —Jack L.

A strong ballerina. –Sloane P.

A UPS driver, embarrassingly so. —Mindy F.

I wanted to be a nurse. Now I want to run a Kona Ice snow cone truck, but really just out of my own driveway. —Julie A.

I wanted to work in a button factory. —Michelle H.

A photojournalist for *National Geographic* or an architect. —Sonya C.

A second-grade teacher. Or a stage actress. —Diane C.

NOTE: More than half of those who answered this question gave two wildly different answers—for example, Rachel's niece would like to grow up to be both a vet AND a cheerleader.

"There lurks, perhaps, in every human heart a desire of distinction, which inclines every man first to hope, and then to believe, that Nature has given him something peculiar to himself."

—Samuel Johnson

What is "peculiar to yourself"? What is the precise combination of things that makes you willfully and beautifully different from the rest of the world, that makes you distinctly you?

I love being an aunt and watching my niece and nephew get older, becoming their own special, little, weird, and wonderful people. This past year, seven-year-old Clara has enjoyed wearing sky blue cat-eye glasses frames (with the lenses popped out), because she thinks her face looks plain without them. Four-year-old Jack loves belting out the lyrics to "Living on a Prayer" at any given moment. When I look at Clara in her cute glasses or Jack hollering out, "Oh-hoh, halfway there..." I wonder, *Who are these people?* I'm excited I'll get to discover the answers with them as they grow.

—Meg

Interview your family and people who knew you when you were young. What strange and awesome things did you do when you were a kid?

Sigmund Freud believed every human's psyche was composed of three separate parts: the ego (your everyday consciousness), your super-ego (the moral, Jiminy Cricket side of you), and your id (your base needs and deepest unrestrained desires).

What do your ego, superego, and id look like? Draw them here.

When my Grandpa Leder passed away, I was surprised to find he kept an autograph book as a teenager. It showed me a whole new side of my stern German grandfather, one in which he was a living, breathing teenager, a person like me. He had a group of friends, each of whom wrote charming or funny rhyming passages in his book, and I marveled at the signatures of people long gone.

The funniest:

Mr. Stillfred Leder:
This is the Fool
who fought a duel
just on the account of a girl
and How.
Fool "Russ"

My favorite, however, is dated October 7, 1934, and is from a woman named Clara.

Dear Stillfred:
On the beautiful Isle of Somewhere,
Far off on life's placid sea,
There are beautiful memories awaiting,
If you remember me.
Clara

There were beautiful memories awaiting, as it turns out, as Clara was my grandma.

—Meg

Research old-fashioned autographs, and create a few signature ones for yourself here. Copy a few of the autographs you've received, whether in yearbooks or letters, and paste them here.

"Life's funny. To a kid, time always drags. Suddenly you're fifty. All that's left of your childhood fits in a rusty little box."

— Amelie

Fill the rusty little box below with drawings and words that encapsulate your childhood.

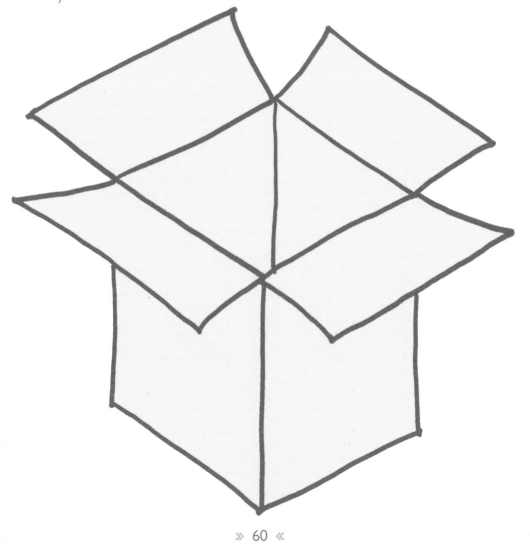

WHAT MAKES YOU LAUGH
WHEN YOU'RE ALONE?

Is a vegetarian permitted to eat animal crackers?

—George Carlin

Collect the fortunes from fortune cookies and paste them here. What does your future hold?

you will receive a fortune (cookie).

CIRCLE ONE:

Morning bird **OR** Night owl?

Salty **OR** Sweet?

Cheese **OR** Chocolate?

Sweet **OR** Sour?

Cats **OR** Dogs?

Ocean **OR** Mountains?

City **OR** Country?

Indoors **OR** Outdoors?

Introvert **OR** Extrovert?

Clean **OR** Messy?

Tortoise **OR** Hare?

Team Edward **OR** Team Jacob?

PC **OR** Mac?

I wasn't bullied much—and that's a good and lucky thing. Even so, I still remember in startling detail every mean incident from elementary school through high school. A few of my bullies have friended me on Facebook, and it's awfully hard for me to get over those twenty-five-year-old slights.

—Rachel

Were you teased or bullied? Were you a bully? Did you witness bullying firsthand? How do you feel about it now?

"Monsters are real, and ghosts are real too. They live inside us and sometimes they win."

— Stephen King

HAVE YOU CONQUERED ANY DEMONS IN YOUR LIFE? HOW?

WHAT HAVE YOU LOST?

WHAT HAVE YOU FOUND?

Has your recollection of your childhood changed? Has it gotten rosier or more realistic over time? Do you see things now that you didn't see then?

"A childhood is what anyone wants to remember of it. It leaves behind no fossils, except perhaps in fiction."

—Carol Shields

morning blend

earl grey

hot chocolate

cappuccino

If you could take anyone from history out to coffee to pick his or her brain, who would it be? What would you ask? Why? (Also, what would you each order?)

"There must be quite a few things a hot bath won't cure, but I don't know many of them."

— Sylvia Plath

 hat are the rituals that bring you most back to yourself, that calm you, that give your working mind a rest? Write them here. Let the list grow.

Take a careful look at your bedroom or kitchen or any room you frequent on a regular basis. Now pretend you're seeing it for the first time. Observe and report. What can you tell about the person who uses this room? What's under the bed? What objects are lying about?

Observations:

Conclusions:

Status updates are like mini-diary entries—short bursts of information about what you're doing/feeling/thinking in the moment. Write a status update for:

• I HOUR FROM NOW •

• 365 DAYS FROM NOW •

• 2 YEARS AND 6 MONTHS FROM NOW •

• 5 YEARS FROM NOW •

• I0 YEARS FROM NOW, ON YOUR BIRTHDAY •

• 20 YEARS FROM NOW •

And now look back—write a status update retroactively from:

• 1 HOUR AGO •

• 365 DAYS AGO •

• 2 YEARS AND 6 MONTHS AGO •

• 5 YEARS AGO •

• 10 YEARS AGO, ON YOUR BIRTHDAY •

• 20 YEARS AGO •

Films and television shows often parody the deep conversations we have in our teens and twenties when we're trying to figure out the world. We wonder if Batman could beat up Superman, if God exists, if we're really just a small speck of dust in a universe of Horton-size elephants.

Recall some of your favorite conversations here. What big questions plagued you when you were younger—and which ones continue to plague you now?

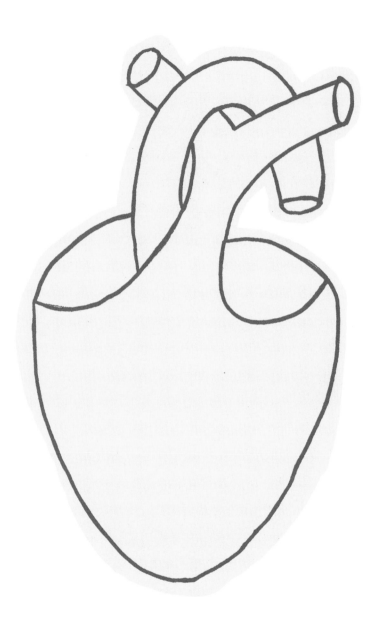

Map the places of your heart. Where do your old crushes live, your favorite people, your secret wishes?

Make yourself a small secret container to hold memories and mementoes. Cookie fortunes that hit the mark. Tiny plastic deer that once rested on your drink glass. A restaurant receipt from the date where everything went right.

You don't need to be a Martha Stewart–caliber crafter to decorate a discarded candy tin or a cigar box. And if you're loathe to craft at all, just buy yourself a fancy special pencil case—it's very easy to hide one in plain sight.

Sketch out your ideas here.

Of course, the best part is finding a place to hide your box. Keep it tucked under your mattress, stashed in your freezer, or, for the adventurous, nestled between the pages of a hollowed-out book.

"Memory is a way of holding on to the things you love, the things you are, the things you never want to lose."

— *The Wonder Years*

When I graduated from high school, I received a small cedar box. I've kept it, filling it with the documents and objects that mean the most to me: a letter from my high school English teacher telling me he thought I'd be a good teacher, a silver egg one of my first loves gave me, the quirky postcards my good friend Candace sends me. Every now and then, I take the box out and let myself linger on the contents, remembering the beautiful moments I've experienced and the people I love. It's like an archive of my inner heart.

—Meg

If you were a reality-show contestant, who would you be? The schemer? The nice one? The fish out of water? The smart one? Or none of the above because you'd never, ever consider being a reality-show contestant?

✱✱✱

Create a list of new holidays that mean something to you: My Cat's Birthday, Best Kiss of My Life Day, Annual Day to Celebrate Spring at the Park, etc. Do something to commemorate each of them when the day arrives.

It's your day to be a superhero. Who are you? What's your secret power? Where are your headquarters? Who is your archnemesis?

» » SECRET SURVEY! « «

IF YOU COULD HAVE A SUPERPOWER, WHAT WOULD IT BE?

I would be able to cure cancer and make my mom well again. —Megan M.

I'd go Wolverine style, no question. Retractable claws! Metallic skeleton! Animal senses! Instant healing! Hugh Jackman's rugged good looks! —Tracey K.

Invisibility—most definitely! —Rebecca F.

To fly like a vulture. Their wings form a "v," and they catch the wind and sail. —Harry C.

The ability to stop time. Sometimes I feel like the world is moving too fast. I'd use my powers for good—prevent a car crash, get the very important assignment done on time—but sometimes I think I'd use them to take a nap. —Katie L.

I would calm animals with a look and allow them to know they are cared for. —Vim P.

Predict winning Lotto numbers. —Jim L.

Flying. Duh. —Alice P.

Make math problems appear, like on *Electric Company*. —Clara L.

Turn people into bunnies. —Ava R.

Jump far like Wonder Woman! —Giavanna C.

NOTE: It's a bird! It's a plane! It's no surprise that more than 60 percent of our survey-takers want to fly!

Print out a few of the pictures you've used in your social media profiles in the past few months. In the space below, describe what you were feeling in the picture. Were you taking the picture yourself and hoping you were catching your face at a good angle? Were you hoping the party would end so you could get home and snuggle up in bed? Try to think back and remember exactly where your mind wandered while you were being snapped.

As a book editor, I've had the privilege of being able to work with Summer Pierre (www.summerpierre.com), an artist, illustrator, writer, and all-around kick-ass gal. Summer is a big believer in making sure your creative life isn't relegated to just after your workday or the weekends. She has a beautiful, bright pink studio and a green kitchen. She draws cool pictures of Phyllis Diller. And in 2011, on her blog, she made a list of 100 things she wants to do in 2011. Her list is awesome, with entries ranging from memorizing a poem to interviewing musician Ani DiFranco to getting a muumuu tailored into a dress. In the entry, she says, "I like the story this list has the POTENTIAL to tell."

—Meg

Taking inspiration from Summer, create your own list. What kind of story does your wish list have the potential to tell?

If you look back at my favorite T-shirts over the years, it's like an archive of who I've been and who I am now: a 1990 Depeche Mode Violator tour shirt, a hot pink shirt from Barcelona with a small felt dog sewn on a pocket, a soft green tee flecked with a flock of white birds, a college volunteer day shirt. I was heartbroken when the Depeche Mode T-shirt finally started to disintegrate but decided not to throw it away yet. Instead, I gathered it and more of my favorite old shirts and made a scarf…cutting out large squares from each and using bright thread to hem the edges. Now, when I wear it, it's like I carry all my favorite memories on my shoulders.

—Meg

MAKE YOUR OWN T-SHIRT SCARF. WHAT YOU'LL NEED:

10-20 favorite old T-shirts
Scissors
Thread

Sewing machine (optional)
Cardboard (for a template)
Iron

1. Start by creating a cardboard template for the size of your squares. I made mine 6 x 6 inches.
2. Using the template, cut out squares from your T-shirts. Place them in a line to determine how long you'd like your scarf to be. Once you have a number in mind, double it, so you have squares for the back of your scarf too.
3. Arrange half the squares in a long line, choosing an order you like. Keep in mind that the squares in the middle will most likely be scrunched around your neck, so put the squares you want to show off near the ends.
4. Sew the squares to each other, using ¼-inch of a seam allowance.
5. Repeat using the other half of the squares.
6. Iron, pressing the seams flat.
7. Place your two lines of scarves on top of each other, patterns facing inward. Sew around the edges, using ¼-inch seam allowance, leaving one top open.
8. Turn your scarf tube inside out, and then sew the remaining opening with a whip stitch.
9. Press flat.
10. Wear!

Look at your browser history for the last month. Now imagine you're a stranger tasked with describing you based just on that information— what would this stranger say about you?

YOU HAVE ONE YEAR TO DO WHATEVER
YOU WANT. WHAT DO YOU DO?

YOU HAVE ONE MONTH TO DO WHATEVER
YOU WANT. WHAT DO YOU DO?

YOU HAVE ONE WEEK TO DO WHATEVER
YOU WANT. WHAT DO YOU DO?

YOU HAVE ONE DAY TO DO WHATEVER
YOU WANT. WHAT DO YOU DO?

YOU HAVE ONE HOUR TO DO WHATEVER
YOU WANT. WHAT DO YOU DO?

YOU HAVE ONE MINUTE TO DO WHATEVER
YOU WANT. WHAT DO YOU DO?

Last year I went on a business trip to London. They put us up in a lovely hotel, and I had a night off to enjoy it. I poured heaps of bubble bath into the soaking tub, grabbed a new book I'd saved for such an occasion, and poured myself a cup of tea (in a real china tea cup). Bath, book, and tea in London? Just thinking about it makes everything better.

—Rachel

Close your eyes for a few minutes and imagine the most relaxing place possible. Is the place you imagine somewhere you've been before or a world you created in your imagination? Describe it here in words or pictures.

Many films and books play with the idea of the butterfly effect—how a seemingly small and insignificant occurrence can lead to a dramatic change in the universe. Was there a small moment in your life that changed everything? Give it a good think and write about it here.

Do you have a secret you've never told another living soul? Write it out here. Then tear out the page and bury it or throw it into the sea or set it ablaze in a campfire.

If you were to write an insider's guide to the place you live, what would you list as the best parts—the things you'd only find in a guidebook written by you? The grilled artichoke hearts at your favorite restaurant? The great vintage jewelry at the local thrift store? The secret garden behind the community bookstore?

If you were a crayon, what color would you be? Draw it here.

If you were a paint swatch, what color would you be? Paste it here.

If you were an ice cream, what kind would you be? Record it here.

If you were a VW Bug, what color would you be? Draw it here.

If you were a font, what type would you be? Record it here.

If you were a shoe, what type would you be? Draw it here.

If you were a _____, what _____ would you be?
Fill in the blanks, and then record the answers here.

Use these pages to log your dreams for the next month. Fingers crossed that you won't have a single nightmare.

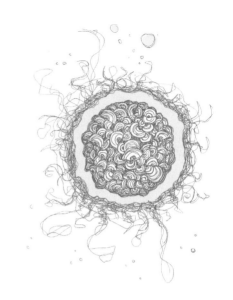

When I was little, on cold days, my mom would make us rice pudding. To this day, it represents comfort and warmth, in the form of plump raisins and the smell of cinnamon. Even now, living twelve hours away from my parents, making rice pudding makes me feel loved and safe— just like home.

—Meg

What food brings you comfort? Why?
Include the recipe here:

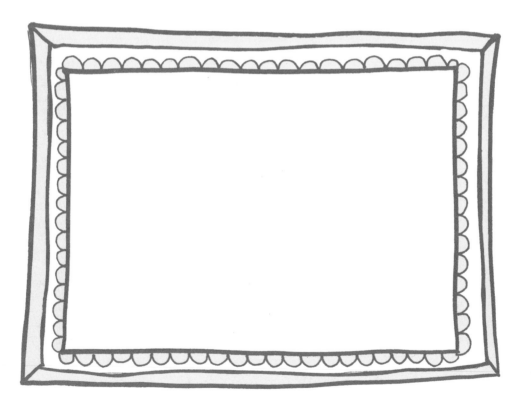

» » SECRET SURVEY! « «

WHAT'S YOUR FAVORITE COMFORT FOOD?

Homemade rhubarb custard pie with a lattice top crust. —Jenny C.

Chipotle and Graeter's Black Raspberry Chip. —Rebecca F.

My mom's lemon meringue pie. —Jim L.

Mac and cheese, hands down. —Micol O.

I'm a chick-flick heroine: Ice Cream. —Jessica C.

Ice cream. Vanilla, of course. —Sabrina A.

Hillstone's French Dip Sandwich. —Matthew B.

French Toast and/or mac and cheese. —Annemarie L.

Perogies! —Julia Y.

Fifteen White Castle burgers. —Dan K.

Stew. —Delaney K.

Candy and pickles but not together. —Sally S.

Spaghetti and meatballs. —Alice M.

Pork chops. —Nancy E.

NOTE: Mac and cheese was the clear-cut winner—followed closely by ice cream. We were surprised that pickles rated so highly! More than five secret survey takers declared their love for the briney spears.

Did you ever have an imaginary friend (or five)? Draw and describe them here. If not, make one up for yourself.

Did you have a secret hiding place when you were a kid? Describe it here.

In my high school journal, I described an idealized version of the perfect boyfriend: a dark-haired Cure fan who always wore Converse. As time went on, my vision changed: someone kind and employed. Older and wiser, right?

—Rachel

H as your vision of your ideal partner changed over time, or has it held steady? Spend some time writing about it here.

WHAT MEMORIES DO YOU COME BACK TO TIME AND AGAIN?

"God gave us memory so that we might have roses in December."

—J. M. Barrie

When I was a kid, I had a shadowbox in my bedroom. I filled each compartment with tiny knickknacks: a miniature figurine that looked like our family cat, a wee painted thimble, a peach pit that had been hand-carved into a tiny basket. It was a perfect place to hold on to small things I loved.

—Meg

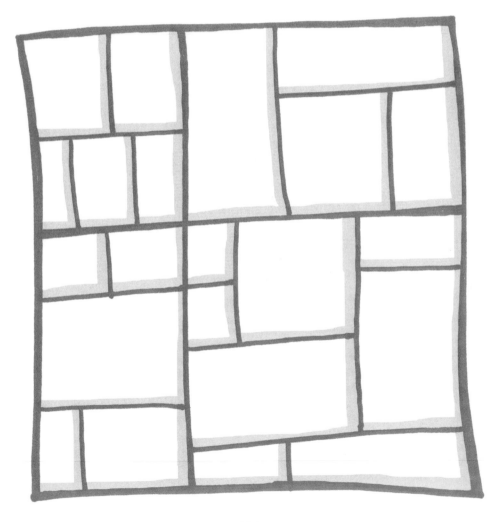

Fill the shadowbox below. Whether you draw objects or write words or paste in pictures, make this the place to hold on to small things you love.

RESEARCH YOUR DATE OF BIRTH

WHAT TIME WERE YOU BORN?

WHAT WAS THE WEATHER LIKE?

WHAT WERE THE HEADLINES IN THE PAPER?

WHAT WAS THE NUMBER ONE SONG ON THE BILLBOARD CHARTS?

WHAT WAS THE MOST POPULAR MOVIE?

"What's in a name? that which we call a rose
By any other name would smell as sweet;
So Romeo would, were he not Romeo call'd,
Retain that dear perfection which he owes
Without that title."

—*Romeo and Juliet*

Research meanings of your name. Record them here. If you feel so inclined, take it a step further and research your name's popularity over time. (Baby name books are a great starting point!)

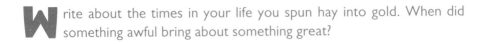

Write about the times in your life you spun hay into gold. When did something awful bring about something great?

Years ago I took a new job—and it was hard! I worked long hours and didn't have many easy days. On the flip side, it's also the place I first met Meg and a heap of other wonderful people.

—Rachel

Have you ever experienced a day so perfectly perfect that you could live it over and over again until the end of time? Write it down here. Include every last detail you can remember.

MY FAVORITE THING SURVEY:

COLOR:

FOOD:

SONG:

MOVIE:

TV SHOW:

PERSON:

ICE CREAM FLAVOR:

PIZZA TOPPING:

BAND:

HOLIDAY:

NUMBER:

LETTER:

GAME:

DRINK:

SPORT:

ANIMAL:

PLACE:

BOOK:

AUTHOR:

ARTIST:

ACTOR:

ACTRESS:

SHOES:

SEASON:

FLOWER:

WEBSITE:

"Raindrops on roses and whiskers on kittens..."

—"My Favorite Things," *The Sound of Music*

"If you look deeply into the palm of your hand, you will see your parents and all generations of your ancestors. All of them are alive in this moment. Each is present in your body. You are the continuation of each of these people."

—Thich Nhat Hanh

 hat do you see of your parents and relatives in you?

What words do you love the sound of, the look of, the meaning of? Bananas? Tertiary? Magnanimous? Shenanigans? Record them here.

Some of the most creative people we know use vision boards to express their hopes and dreams for the future. Sometimes the board reflects something deep and difficult and specific—a fight against cancer or the hope for a child. Sometimes it's a bit more prosaic—a hope for a happier future or a desire to make more time for creative endeavors. Vision boards can be a positive force, a call to action and a bit of hopefulness on days when life is hard. They are always about looking ahead to a brighter, happier, better future.

—Rachel

V ision boards are traditionally used to look ahead—but what about creating a vision board full of mementos and photos and symbols of the great things you've already accomplished and hurdles you've already overcome? Across these two pages, paste in mementos of your achievements, observations, and photos—anything that celebrates those wonderful things you've already done.

"Everyone is a moon, and has a dark side which he never shows to anybody."

—Mark Twain

Describe the darker side of you. What about that dark side, as poet Wendell Berry put it, "blooms and sings"?

In college, I worked at a coffee shop. As anyone who's ever worked customer service can attest, you get your fair share of weirdos, jerks, and mean people. Whenever I was confronted with a person in a terrible mood, I imagined what it would be like to throw fruit at them…maybe a quick barrage of grapes at the forehead, or an apple plunked on the side of the temple. Yes, it was a totally bizarre coping mechanism, but it got me (and the customers) through the day intact.

—Meg

WHAT ARE YOUR PRIVATE COPING MECHANISMS?

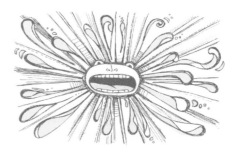

Have someone take a full length picture of you and paste it below. On the opposite page, call out certain things about yourself, as if you were being included in a "Person on the Street" magazine feature, e.g. "Haircut at Bumble & Bumble," "Scarf was a gift from my Aunt Judy," "My most beloved gym shoes."

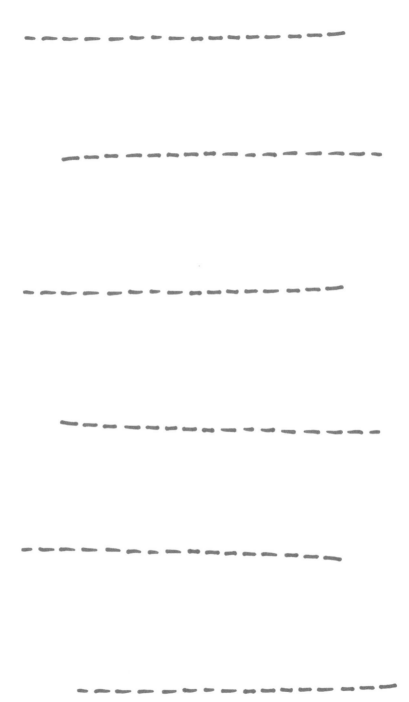

In my neighborhood woods, up a steep dirt hill and behind a thicket of ·
bushes, sat an abandoned family cemetery. It was a peaceful, magic-
feeling place, and I spent summer afternoons imagining who was buried
there. I rarely had more to go on than names and dates, but that was
all I needed to imagine family dramas and lives lived before I was born.

—Rachel

What would you like to have inscribed on your tombstone? Something
earnest, deep, cryptic, or funny? Plan your epitaph here.

"The best time for planning a book is while you're doing the dishes."

—Agatha Christie

What kind of book would you write if you had the time and the talent? A memoir? A book of silly poems? A history of cupcakes?

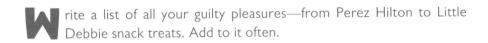**W**rite a list of all your guilty pleasures—from Perez Hilton to Little Debbie snack treats. Add to it often.

DO YOU HAVE ANY GUILTY PLEASURES?

Watching *The Jersey Shore*—I just feel better about my own life watching that train wreck of a show. —Becky F.

Totino's Pizza Rolls. (I hide them under healthier fare in my shopping cart when I succumb to the urge.) Cheese and meat and grease wrapped up in a little bite-sized crust. Double yum. —Michelle T.

Reading baseball blogs. —Jack H.

Shoes, ice cream, and Nickelodeon. —Allie S.

My favorite thing to watch when I'm down are old episodes of *Saved By the Bell*, because that show was and will always be awesome. —Ann D.

Watching television for teen viewers. —Donya D.

Eating raw cookie dough by the roll. —Heather R.

Ice cream (full fat). Why scrimp? —Mallika P.

Stealthily reading over strangers' shoulders on the subway. —Mindy F.

Chocolate chip muffins. —Elise T.

Staying in my PJs as long as possible. —Judy S.

Ed from *Gossip Girl*. —Annemarie L.

Ice cream, pickles, chocolate, the Internet, true crime stories, and *The Price is Right*. —Kambri C.

NOTE: There are an awful lot of grown-ups in the world who enjoy TV and books made for teens! (We're looking at you, *Vampire Diaries*.)

Grab an ink pad and record your unique fingerprints. Note and label the whorls and loops that form your own particular signature.

tented arch

plain whorl

double loop

accidental

plain arch

loop

central pocket loop

"Each one of you has something no one else has, or has ever had: your fingerprints, your brain, your heart. Be an individual. Be unique. Stand out. Make noise. Make someone notice. That's the power of individuals."

—Jon Bon Jovi

At the end of the film *Titanic*, Rose decides to abandon the life of affluence (and misery) she knew and build a new life with a new name in America.

Imagine starting your life over from scratch. How would you begin? What would you change? Who would you become?

Many of Emily Dickinson's poems weren't published in her lifetime. However, after her death, her sister found forty small, handbound booklets in Emily's belongings. Each featured different poems, bound together with string. The books have come to be known as "fascicles"—bundles or clusters.

Create your own fascicle. Take twenty pieces of 8½ by 11 paper, and fold them in half. Staple them at the crease (or if you're feeling especially ambitious, sew the crease with thread, using a thick needle). Fill the pages of your book, and then hide it for someone else to find…soon or years from now.

BOOK IDEAS:

Your favorite quotes
Your grocery list, illustrated
Sentences and phrases you overhear
TV character aliases
Cats you have loved
Totally unsatisfying desserts
The best birthday you have ever had
[Your name] and the terrible, horrible, no good,
very bad day (a homage to Alexander!)

cats I have loved

Most workdays, I start my morning by taking a fifteen-minute walk to the subway. Every morning, there are things I like to look for along the way: the black-and-white stray cat nestled in the corner of a vacant lot, cool shoes in the window of the shoe store, the typo in the sign of the vegan restaurant (Aslan Vegan vs. Asian Vegan—and then I like to imagine the lion from Narnia opening a vegan restaurant). There are also things that surprise me: new quirky graffiti, the day the snow was as high as the parking meters, a man singing randomly at the top of his lungs.

—Meg

Spend some time observing what you see when you walk. Record the impressions here. Do it again—a day later, a week later, a month later. Create a visual record of the world only you and you alone can create.

What would be your perfect grocery shopping list if calories and cost were no option?

◄ tacos ◄ cupcakes ◄ pizza ◄ spagettio's ◄ skyline ◄ strawberries ◄

◄ heirloom tomatoes ◄ artichoke hearts ◄ hot chocolate ◄ chimichurri ◄

WHAT PARTICULAR
THINGS GROSS YOU OUT?

Things Meg cannot handle: Shoes that look like feet, Tom Hanks movies, tapioca pudding, when people wear tights as if they're pants.

Things Rachel cannot handle: People eating on the subway, tuna fish juice, the smell of gingko trees.

When I was a wee lass, I had an epiphany: Root beer and pretzels were the perfect afternoon snack. From that point on, I spent years plotting and planning a chain of root beer and pretzel mall kiosks. Honestly, I'm still convinced it's a genius idea.

—Rachel

If you could open a store, what would you sell? Sketch out a business plan below.

"…it's hard to stay mad when there's so much beauty in the world. Sometimes I feel like I'm seeing it all at once, and it's too much. My heart fills up like a balloon that's about to burst…And then I remember… to relax and not try to hold on to it. And then it flows through me like rain. And I can't feel anything but gratitude for every single moment of my stupid little life."

—American Beauty

Looking back at your life, what beauty has existed in your world? What things are you grateful for in your "stupid little life"? What simple things fill you with awe?

What are the places you always wanted to visit? Imagine you can go to all of them. Paste a map of your journey here, and write out your dream itinerary in as much detail as you can imagine. (Pretend time, money, and other reality-based travel constraints aren't an issue!)

MAP

MY DREAM ITINERARY

Jamie Ridler is one of our favorite people. Through her website and podcast and speaking engagements, she encourages everyone to be courageous and creative and inspired. Her website (http://jamieridlerstudios.ca/) is a little bit magical. The prompt that follows is from the mind of Jamie—we hope you'll like it as much as we do.

—Rachel & Meg

Ever since I was a pre-teen, I've loved magazines. I've tucked hundreds (maybe thousands!) of their glossy pics into my journals. Looking back, the constants are clear: my love of drama, cool colors, clear glass, circles.

Grab your favorite magazine and tear out a picture that tugs at your heart. Trust your instincts. Glue it here. Add some thoughts about why this picture spoke to you. What does it reveal?

Who are the people you've loved the most? Fill these pages with photos, stories, and quotes from the people who have made the biggest impact on your life.

When I was in college, my friends Eric and Terry and I spontaneously decided to go see a midnight showing of a Quentin Tarantino movie. While I can't remember which film we saw, I do remember the night was chilly, and Eric let me borrow one of his favorite sweatshirts: gray, with slightly ragged cuffs. I loved wearing it, being warm, seeing the movie with two of my favorite people, and so I selfishly kept the sweatshirt. Eric has never asked for it back, and for that I am grateful; anytime I need to feel the comfort of good friends, I wear it.

—Meg

For you, what item of clothing is made of more than just thread and fabric? Why? What else does it encompass?

Go online and research your astrological sign. Write down the traits associated with your sign. Now write your own horoscope for the year that is to come. What hopes and dreams do you have for yourself? What good things await you?

In *Ferris Bueller's Day Off,* Ferris and his friends Cameron and Sloane play hooky and visit the Chicago Art Museum. Cameron spends time studying Seurat's *A Sunday Afternoon on the Island of La Grande Jatte,* staring at the small girl in the middle, focusing closer and closer on her face until it becomes just small dots. It's a unique moment of calm in an otherwise hilarious, frenetic movie, but it speaks to Cameron's quest for self-identity, his desire to become his own person.

What piece of art speaks to you? Why? Paste a picture of it here. Learn everything you can about the piece and the artist, and record it here. Then, try to capture why it speaks to you.

What do you spend most of your free time doing: texting, watching TV, reading, talking on the phone? Once you've identified your biggest free-time habit, try going without it for three days. Record the results here. Does absence make the heart grow fonder? What new interests emerge?

What embarrassing moments can you reclaim? Practice the art of laughing at yourself. Record an incident you're ready to move past below, and then learn to start laughing at it. Share it with a friend who can always make you laugh.

In high school, my friend Rachel was notorious for having truly embarrassing scrapes. Yet, she always good-naturedly shared the stories of her mishaps with me and our friends Candace, Julie, and Alyssa, turning them into occasions for laughter. Years later, we still fondly retell these "Rachel Stories." And years later, I'm still in awe of how Rachel can laugh at herself and how she reclaims her embarrassment by generously sharing the laughter with us.

—Meg

I have a goofy tradition of taking photos of my niece and nephew making faces. They step in front of the camera, and I shout out directions. We start simple: "You're happy!" and then get more ridiculous: "You're being chased by a bear, but it's your birthday, and the bear is wearing a tiny party hat." When we're done, I have dozens of silly photos capturing every possible face the kids can make.

—Rachel

Take pictures of yourself making every kind of face imaginable—sad, happy, excited, shocked, miserable, ecstatic—and then examine the results. Which photos look the most convincing? Are you better at faking happiness or sadness or something in between? Write about it here—then paste in your favorite pictures from the photo shoot.

"I loathe the expression 'What makes him tick.' It is the American mind, looking for simple and singular solution, that uses the foolish expression. A person not only ticks, he also chimes and strikes the hour, falls and breaks and has to be put together again, and sometimes stops like an electric clock in a thunderstorm."

—James Thurber

Do you tick? If so, what gets you ticking? Or do you chime and strike the hour? If so, what stops you like an electric clock in a thunderstorm?

In kindergarten, MaryKate won the fire department poster contest, and in sixth grade, David won writer of the year. I am still not fully over either affront.

—Rachel

Do you harbor a jealous grudge from childhood? What does this say about your younger self?

Some things in life earn us accolades—graduating from high school, saving a kitten from a tree, getting a promotion at work. Use these pages to brag about the small things that don't get recognized so readily—getting up early to go to the gym, finishing a project ahead of time, making a delicious dinner, or calling your grandma every Sunday without fail for a year. Keep adding to the list. Paste in more pages if you run out of room.

"Secrets are things we give to others to keep for us."

—Elbert Hubbard

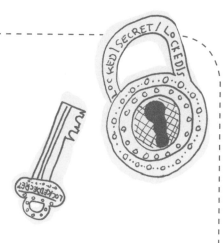

It can be hard to keep other people's secrets, and sometimes we all feel like we have to get them out. Do it here…write everything you're holding in for other people. Once you've got it all out of your system, cover it up. Make a collage with magazine pictures or torn pieces of construction paper or old notes from friends. Take a black Sharpie marker and cover over the entire thing. Undo the secret telling.

I once went out with a guy who, the first time he came to my apartment, rudely shoved my sleeping cat off a chair so he could sit down. It was, as Liz Lemon would say, a deal-breaker.

—Meg

WHAT QUALITIES ARE DEAL-BREAKERS FOR YOU?

I met Candace on our first day of high school. She had a copy of *Anne of Green Gables* sticking out of her bag. I figured anyone who loved that book enough to carry around high school would be a kindred spirit. I was right. She turned out to be one of my best friends.

—Meg

WHAT QUALITIES ARE DEAL-MAKERS FOR YOU?

If you had to grab one thing from your home and never return, what would it be and why?

» » SECRET SURVEY! « «

IF YOU COULD ONLY TAKE ONE ITEM FROM YOUR HOUSE BEFORE LEAVING YOUR HOME FOREVER, WHAT WOULD IT BE (NOT COUNTING PEOPLE AND PETS!)?

The lamp that my great-great-aunt handpainted. —Pat L.

My wedding picture. I wouldn't go anywhere without my wedding picture. —Harry C.

My lucky coins. —Jessica R.

Blanket (soft blanky). —Jack L.

Clean underwear. No matter where you go, you're always going to need clean underwear. —Jessica C.

Lip balm. —Elise T.

My children's adoption information, which includes the only pictures they will probably ever have of their birth mothers. —Julie A.

My grandma's tea cups. —Amy C.

The stuffed dog my aunt got me. —Delaney K.

My son's wedding album. —Karen K.

My stuffed bear named Beary that I recently rescued from my parent's house. He's still soft. —Julee S.

A picture of my kids holding hands. —Jenn R.

NOTE: 75 percent of people gave us incredibly practical answers: laptops and hard drives and iPhones. The other 25 percent went for the sentimental quilts, family photos, and beloved stuffed toys.

What is the thing you're most looking forward to today, right at this moment?

"Each has his past shut in him like the leaves of a book shown to him by heart, and his friends can only read the title."

—Virginia Woolf

WHAT IS THE TITLE
OF YOUR MEMOIR?

Pretend you're in a space entirely by yourself. Perhaps it's a subway car, and you're swiftly hurtling through dark underground tunnels. Or maybe you're in a deep forest, pine trees all around you. Draw where you are below. What would you say out loud in this space of total privacy?

Every now and then, I end up in a totally empty subway car for a stop or two, which is a rarity in New York City. When I have those moments, I let myself say, out loud, something secret about myself.

—Meg

BOOKS I WANT TO READ:

RESTAURANTS AND FOODS I WANT TO TRY:

PLACES I WANT TO GO:

THINGS I WANT TO SEE:

Your soul mate is out in the world right now…who is he or she, what are they doing, where do they live, how will you meet? Or have you already met? Write all about your soul mate here.

"The idea of her life shall sweetly creep
Into his study of imagination…"

—William Shakespeare

Look over the shoes you've had through the years. Chronicle your life history through them: Your favorite pair of gym shoes when you were a kid, your first pair of Doc Martens when you were going through a rebellious stage, a particularly great (but uncomfortable) pair of dress shoes for your first formal dance, the vintage cowboy boots you bought for a first date. Include a visual record here.

Trees grow in layers from the inside out, adding a new ring of growth every year. When you see these cross-sections, you're seeing a history of the tree's life. You can determine how old it is based on how many rings there are. Some rings may be wider, depending on the abundance of water that year, and you can also determine if a tree survived a forest fire.

If you were a tree, what would the history of your life look like? Draw the cross-section here. Label years of abundance and events you've lived through.

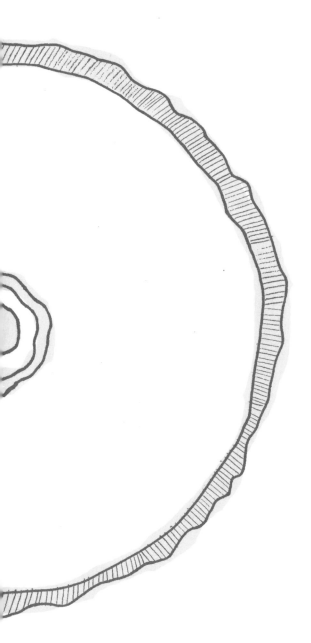

I slept with Snowball the teddy bear for twenty years. I didn't spend a night without him until I left grad school—he was packed into luggage and dragged onto planes well into my adulthood. He started off white and ended up gray despite repeated washings on the gentle cycle. He was, without exception, the most well-loved toy I ever had.

—Rachel

What was your favorite childhood toy? Who gave it to you? Did you love it deeply for a short while, or carry it with you from kindergarten to college? If you have a picture, paste it here.

» » SECRET SURVEY! « «

WHAT IS/WAS YOUR FAVORITE CHILDHOOD TOY?

Either Richard Scary's Puzzle Town or my Weeble Wobble Tree House. —Rebecca F.

Flippy, my gray hippo. I've had her since I was 3. —Sonya C.

Fashion Plates! —Jessica R.

Bertha Bunny, who my dad put in my bed at the hospital the day I was born. I still sleep with her, except my cat attacks her. —Katherine L.

Light Bright (Shiny! Glowy! Colorful pegs! I ate a peg once and sadly found out that they didn't glow in your belly). —Vim P.

My Tiny Tears doll. —Karen K.

We had an old beat-up metal rickshaw that my dad would take my brother and me in for walks around the neighborhood. Needless to say, we stopped traffic in it. —Amy F.

My doll Cindy (named after my hero, Cindy on *The Brady Bunch*). At some point, she became completely bald, but I loved her so much, she's still in the guest room closet at my parents' house. —Shana C.

My Transformers. I can't just pick one! —Craig M.

My imagination. The thing I remember most when I was a kid was all the "roleplaying" (though we didn't call it that) games. We'd be mad scientists in Dawn's basement, experimenting on "brains" (twisted--up old towels), or archeologists (I'm sure my parents loved the holes in the yard). —Nancy L.

Matchbox Cars. —Matthew B.

NOTE: Barbies, Barbies, Barbies. And stuffed animals...definitely the most popular responses.

In college, my friend Marla used to say that if she were queen of the world, she'd implement three worldwide rules: (1) Everyone would have to take a parenting class before they could have kids. (2) Everyone would have to work retail during the holiday season for once in their life. (3) No one could wear "Coed Naked" T-shirts anywhere, ever again. Period.

— Meg

IF YOU RULED THE WORLD,
WHAT THREE THINGS WOULD YOU DEMAND?

1.

2.

3.

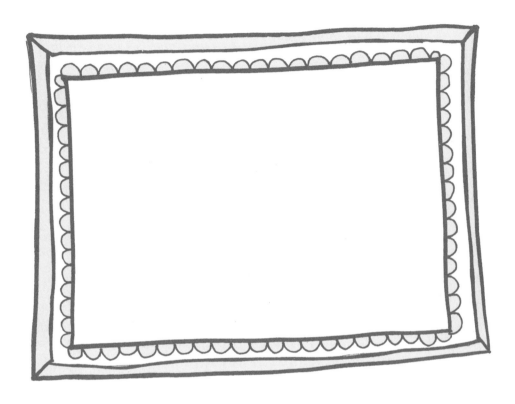

Use the frame above to create a sign that reminds you to be yourself. Come up with a motto or slogan or statement, and decorate it. Cut it out and hang it where you can see it.

"To be nobody but yourself in a world which is doing its best, night and day, to make you everybody else means to fight the hardest battle which any human being can fight; and never stop fighting."

—e.e. cummings

When I meet someone new at a summertime party, it's inevitable that I'll tell her my air conditioner story. It's my stock anecdote. Why? Because I'm one of those people who knocked their air conditioner out of a window. (No one was hurt, but my ego was mightily bruised).

—Rachel

W hat are the stock stories you share with people you've just met? Is there a story you pull out at every party?

I used to love *Bartlett's Familiar Quotations*. It brimmed with wisdom! And I was a little bit of a geek. Now it's easy to find quotes about anything with a quick Google search—and I do that more than I'd like to admit.

—Rachel

Dig a little deeper than *Bartlett's* and Google, and look for quotes about something that matters to you. The kind of "big" ideas that we don't talk about over the coffee pot at work—loyalty, love, friendship, happiness. Write your favorite quotes here.

"How are you going to spend this one odd and precious life you have been issued? Whether you're going to spend it trying to look good and creating the illusion that you have power over people and circumstances, or whether you are going to taste it, enjoy it, and find out the truth about who you are."

—Anne Lamott

If you could do anything with your life, what would it be? Sky's the limit. Would you create a sea turtle sanctuary in Costa Rica? Would you be the first astronaut to walk on Mars? Would you write a novel that fills people with awe? Would you raise a beautiful child who brings you joy?

WHAT DO YOU WISH WERE TRUE?

"I wish I could write as mysterious as a cat."

—Edgar Allan Poe

"If you wake up at a different time, in a different place, could you wake up as a different person?"

—Chuck Palahniuk

WHAT DO YOU THINK...COULD YOU?
WHO WOULD IT BE?
IF NOT, WHY?

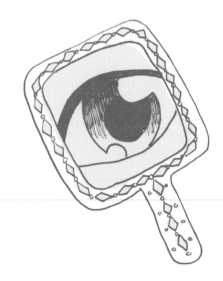

It's time to create the dream cast for the movie of your life. Who would play you, your family and friends, enemies and loves?

Use this space to sketch out the timeline of your life from this day onward. Include practical details (I'll turn 50!) along with your hopes and dreams. Be as serious or silly as you wish.

Whenever I need to feel a song that stirs my heart, I listen to the Waterboys' "Fisherman's Blues." If I want to be reminded of the promise of spring, I listen to the Innocence Mission's album *Glow*. Quiet, mellow rainy days are for Elliot Smith. After one of my favorite people in the world, Mary Mitchell, passed away, Patty Griffin's "Mary" was on nonstop play on my iPod. And when I want to dance, of course I listen to "I Don't Feel Like Dancing" by the Scissor Sisters.

—Meg

List your soul soundtrack—the songs that you come back to time and again for comfort, affirmation, solace, and joy.

»» SECRET SURVEY! ««

NAME A SONG YOU COULD LISTEN TO 1,000 TIMES.

"Dancing Queen" by ABBA. So cheesy, but it brings back fond memories from all stages of my life. —Mallika P.

"Superstition" by Stevie Wonder. —Candace M.

"Your Song" by Elton John. —Judy S.

"Never Been to Spain" by Elvis (the live version at the 1972 Madison Square Garden Concert). —Jenny C.

"This Old Cowboy" by Asleep at the Wheel. —Jack H.

"Alone in Kyoto" by Air. —Jessica R.

"Adult Education" by Hall & Oates or "Dirty Diana" by Michael Jackson. —Kendra H.

"Slide Away," performed by Oasis. The first time I heard it, the huge guitar and the straining vocals and the tortured lyrics just blew the top of my head off. Fifteen years later, it still does. —Katherine L.

"Twinkle Twinkle Little Star" —Sloane P.

"Moonlight Serenade" by Glenn Miller. —Harry C.

Twinkle, Twinkle, Little Star. —James F.

Anything by Justin Bieber. —Sydney K.

NOTE: "Beast of Burden" by The Rolling Stones showed up more than a few times on our surveys!

This book is about all the secret parts of yourself...and while it's good—essential, even—to keep some of these parts just for you, every now and then, it's good to share them. What secrets do you want to share? What do you wish people knew about you? Write them here. Then make a point of introducing that part of your secret self to a good friend. He or she will be happy to meet you.

This is your book, about your secret self. Now it's time to write your own prompt and answer it.

EPILOGUE

"And remember, no matter where you go, there you are."

—Confucius

There. You've done it. For 200 pages, you examined yourself like a scientist, a therapist, a detective, and a scholar. You looked under your bed and inside your heart. You considered improbable things and everyday things. You made an altar, plotted a magical vacation, and looked at yourself in a new way. You stopped the world and turned your time and attention inward.

Now that you're reacquainted with yourself, how do you feel? Was thinking about your secret self a challenge? Was it fun? Surprising? Sad? Is the "you" that started the book the same "you" who finished it?

Meg and I hope the process of reading and writing and thinking about your secret self was a good one—whether it was easy or a struggle. If this book affirmed what you already suspected, that's great. And if it shocked and surprised you, that's great too. Knowledge is power, right? If you've lost a bit of your youthful hopefulness or tamped down the part of you that loves to draw and make things, you can change it. You can take 15 minutes a day or 30 minutes on a Sunday morning to do the things that satisfy and nurture and honor your secret self.

Like Meg, I went through a tough spell too. My dad passed away after a long illness in late 2010. For a long time I was shaken and lost and not feeling like me at all. I marched along and went to work and did the things that needed to be done. Then I started working on this book, and in the process, I remembered that a shaken me is still ME. I'm a little more flaky, a little more antisocial, a little slower to come up with a clever quip, but I will always maintain my inner Rachelness—maker of almost-good crafts, aunt extraordinaire, loyal (albeit erratic) friend, voracious reader, and lover of cats. Even when the glass is really, truly, half empty, I try to imagine it half full.

Thanks for taking the time to honor, remember, examine, and investigate your secret self. Don't stop now. Keep thinking, hoping, dreaming, and doing things that mean something to you. Don't just take time to smell the roses, take time to grow your own roses. Make time for the good things. Make time for good people who nurture and love the real you.

We hope you had as rewarding a time finishing the book as we had writing the book for you. Save it. Read it when you're feeling lost or happy or sad. Find it when you need a little reminder about who you are and what you're made of. It's good stuff—don't forget it. We hope you had as rewarding a time doing it as we had writing the book for you.

—Rachel

ACKNOWLEDGMENTS

Many, many thanks to Shana Drehs for her enthusiasm for our projects; Michael Bourret for being a kick-ass agent and even better friend; Jamie Ridler for her passion for creative living; the kids at the Longwood School District for sharing their wishes; and our friends and family for literally being the best people we know. We are lucky to have them.

ABOUT THE AUTHORS

RACHEL KEMPSTER lives in New York City with her two cats, Foster and Cupcake. Here are some things that make up her secret me: in high school, she drove to Connecticut to see They Might Be Giants without telling her parents (sorry, Mom!), she's a newly minted member of the 501st Legion (which means she really likes *Star Wars*), she slept with a teddy bear named Snowball for twenty years, and she celebrated her eighteenth birthday in a hot air balloon with her grandma.

MEG LEDER lives in Brooklyn, New York, with a cat named after *Friday Night Light's* Tim Riggins. Here are some things that make up her secret me: sometimes she eats unheated SpaghettiO's out of the can; she and her friend Jenny once chased two *Glee* cast members down the street; she wishes she could roller skate around NYC like Olivia Newton John's character from *Xanadu*, be as erudite as Tim Gunn, and have hair like Kate Winslet; and if she were living during the 1920s, her name would have been Maxine.

A not-so-secret thing? Meg and Rachel are also the authors of *The Happy Book*.

it's **your** happiness—
in a book.

THE
HAPPY
BOOK

a journal to celebrate
what makes you happy

Rachel Kempster
Meg Leder

Packed with creative and quirky prompts,
ideas, and activities, **The Happy Book**
gives you an easy way to put a happy smile on your face.

Scribble thoughts, make lists, paste pictures, doodle, and
dream about whatever makes you glad.
(Think...hot chocolate with churros. '80s hair bands.
The first snowfall of the year!)
You'll create your own personal pick-me-up
that you can flip through whenever you want.

It's your happy book—discover and
celebrate all the things (both big and small)
that make you happy.

Goodbye!